D1175793

Illustrations by
Giulia De Amicis

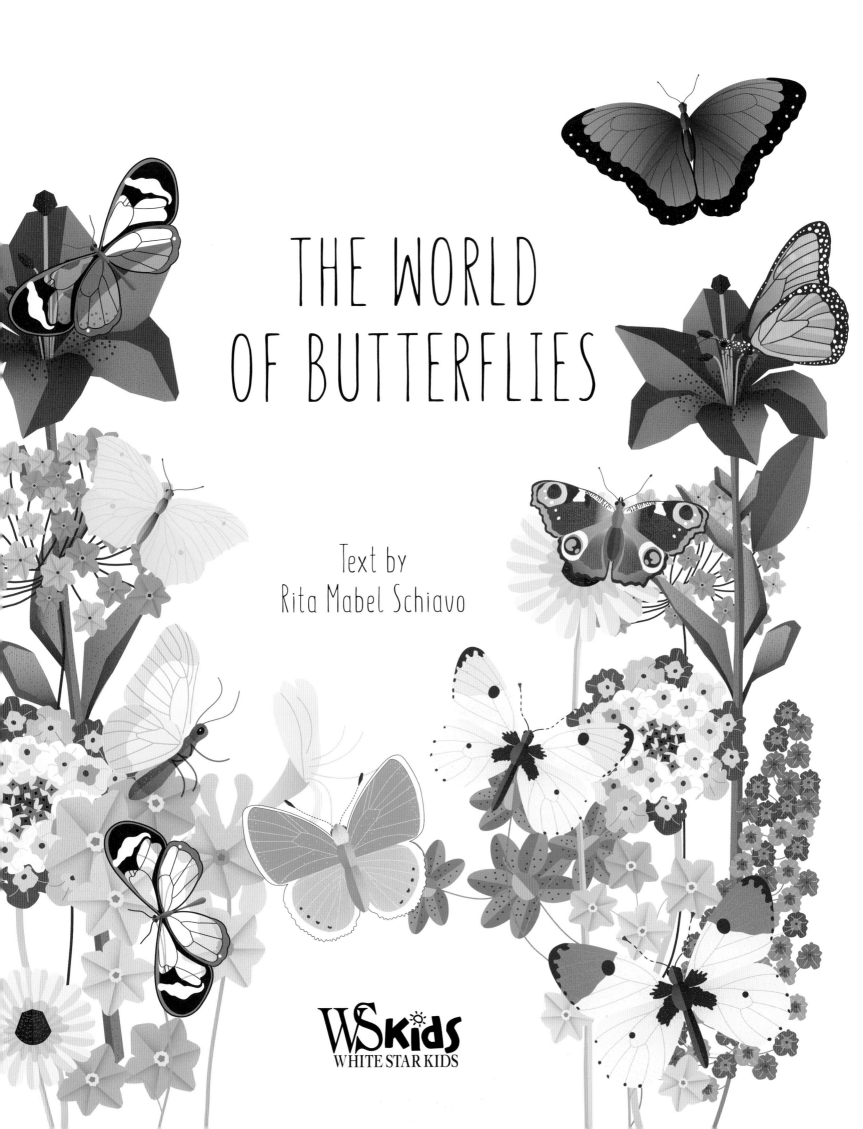

THE WORLD
OF BUTTERFLIES

Text by
Rita Mabel Schiavo

WSKids
WHITE STAR KIDS

Contents

6   Introduction

10   Butterflies

12   Butterfly or moth?

14   Big or small

20   Lepidopterans in the world

22   Anatomy of a butterfly

24   Wings and flight

26   Sense organs

30   How long does a butterfly live?

34   Mating and reproduction

36   Social behavior

40   Camouflage and defense strategies

44   Butterflies and man

46   Conservation

48   The silkworm

50   Raising butterflies

52   Butterfly gardens

54   Myths and legends

56   List of butterflies encountered

in this book

HOW WELL DO YOU REALLY KNOW BUTTERFLIES?

There are animals that nourish themselves sipping a sweet drink through a **STRAW**, that can smell scents **WITHOUT HAVING A NOSE**, that don't have ears but can perceive **SOUNDS** and **ULTRASOUNDS**, that can locate a tiny object among the leaves of a forest. What animals are these? Easy: **BUTTERFLIES!**

BUT A BUTTERFLY IS SO MUCH MORE!

You've seen them countless times flying during the day in **FIELDS IN BLOOM** or in the evening around a **LAMP!** Elegant and often almost impalpable, they seem to belong to some **FAIRYTALE PLACE!**

WOULD YOU LIKE TO COME IN AND VISIT THEIR EXTRAORDINARY LITTLE WORLD?

This book wishes to take you on a journey through their **WORLD**, which is sort of **MAGICAL**, to unveil the many **SECRETS** that the different species hide.

WHERE DOES MAGIC COME IN?

You will discover what the famous "**MAGIC POWDER**" on their wings is and what it's actually needed for: if it remains on our fingers, we have certainly **DAMAGED** the structure of the wing, which is quite delicate, and the insect **WILL NO LONGER BE ABLE TO FLY** and find food.

HAVE YOU EVER WONDERED HOW A CATERPILLAR TURNS INTO A BUTTERFLY?

During part of the journey you will be fascinated by the transition from **CATERPILLAR**, always hungry and chubby, to **MAGNIFICENT BUTTERFLY**, passing through the pupa stage: upon emerging from the cocoon, each individual will begin to spread its wings exactly **LIKE A FLOWER** in bloom and in little time will undertake its **FIRST FLIGHT**.

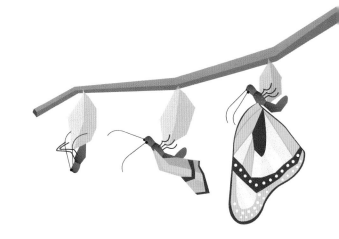

Once metamorphosis is complete, the males, attracted by the exciting scents of the females, will give their all in **SPECTACULAR DANCES** to beat their rivals and conquer the heart of a fiancé that, in some species, will start to **DANCE WITH HER PARTNER.**

You will read about the intelligent **DEFENSE STRATEGIES** of these apparently fragile insects, the positive and negative **RELATIONSHIP** they have had and have with **MAN**, from the **PARASITES** that sneak into pantries to **SILKWORMS.**

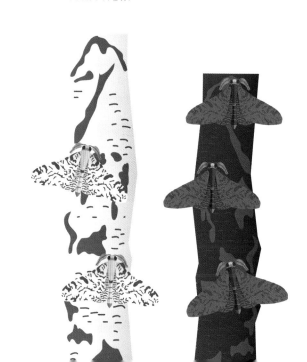

UNFORTUNATELY, ALL FAIRYLAND PLACES ARE AT RISK

COLLECTORS who hunt them, deforestation, extensive farming, and **INSECTICIDES** are leading to a steady decrease in the number of these marvelous insects that we cannot afford to lose.

REMEMBER THAT, WITHOUT THEM, MANY PLANTS COULDN'T BE POLLINATED, CAUSING SERIOUS HARM TO BIODIVERSITY.

For this reason, in the final part of the book you will find some suggestions on how to help and raise butterflies to set free and... **FLY WITH THEM INTO THE REALM OF THE IMAGINATION!**

ENJOY YOUR READING!

1. BUTTERFLIES

We see them fly gracefully from flower to flower with their colorful wings: they are butterflies, the most admired and collected insects; crucial as they are, just like bees, for plant pollination, we have only just recently started to protect them because their numbers are significantly decreasing.

HEAD: sense organs

THORAX: organs for movement

ABDOMEN: digestive and reproductive organs

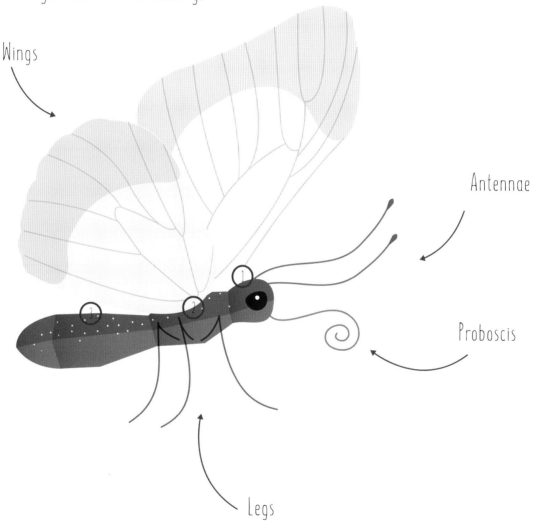

Wings

Antennae

Proboscis

Legs

ANATOMY OF A BUTTERFLY

As all insects, butterflies have a body divided in three sections: head, thorax, and abdomen. On the head, along with the mouthparts, there are a pair of antennae and large compound eyes. Located on the thorax are the organs for movement: four wings and six legs, the standard number within the insect group.

Inside the abdomen are lodged the digestive organs and, primarily, those for reproduction. On the sides of the thorax and abdomen we can observe some tiny holes: these are the spiracles that, connecting to inner tubes, tracheae and tracheoles, make up the respiratory system.

THE EXOSKELETON

The entire body, wings included, is shielded by a firm cuticle that gives support and protection. This exoskeleton is made of chitin, a substance made up mainly of sugars, similar to the cellulose of plants. In order to move, the legs are articulated in many jointed segments such as those of robots.

MULTI-FUNCTION WINGS

Coming in various shapes and colors, butterfly wings are the instruments that not only enable to cover long distances in search of new food sources or a partner, but also to communicate with members of the same species and with predators. The patterns, taken as a whole, correspond to a sort of identity card and are the result of a myriad of tiny scales, commonly called "powder". This is why entomologists have given butterflies the scientific name of Lepidoptera, that is, having wings provided with scales.

The wings, with their intricate patterns, are the butterfly's identity card.

ORIGIN

The origin of lepidopterans is still a matter of study, but the very well preserved fossil of an extinct species, *Prodryas persephone*, tells us that 40 million years ago in North America there flew butterflies that looked just like those we know today. Paleontologists have discovered similar insects that 165 million years ago would go in search of sugary substances on plants that hadn't yet developed actual flowers: it is likely that they had a much older ancestor in common with today's butterflies, which instead appeared only around thirty million years later.

2. BUTTERFLY OR MOTH?

Despite it no longer being considered a correct scientific classification, what falls under the name lepidopteran can be divided into two groups: butterflies and moths. This distinction is in fact still used by entomologists for practical reasons. After all, the differences can be easily observed even by beginner researchers.

If we consider that there are about 170,000 species of Lepidoptera, about 153,000, that is 9 out of 10, are actually moths!

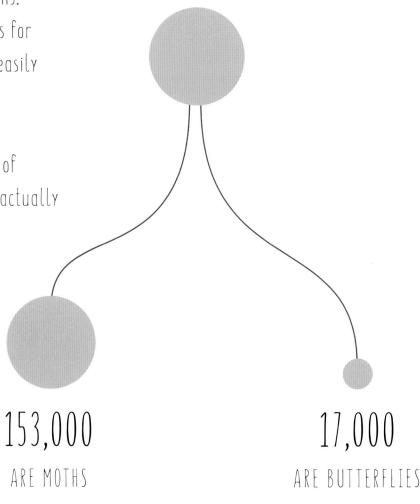

170,000
SPECIES OF LEPIDOPTERANS

153,000
ARE MOTHS

17,000
ARE BUTTERFLIES

THE BODY

While the body of butterflies appears smooth and slim, the body of moths is chubby and furry.

butterfly

moth

THE ANTENNAE

Butterflies have antennae that are thicker on the tips, ending in a sort of bell clapper or flat disk, and for this reason they are described as being "clubbed".

In moths, antennae vary a lot in shape and length. In some groups they are threadlike and can be 5 times the length of the body (genus *Adela*), but often they resemble combs (*Saturnidae*) and have an oval, sword, or spear-like shape. Finally, in certain species they are so thin and disorderly that they look like tiny bird feathers.

THE WINGS

The greatest difference can be seen when the insect is still. In fact, butterflies at rest tend to fold their wings behind their back. There is often a remarkable difference between top side and bottom side: bright colors on top and camouflage underneath.

This way, when the butterfly rests, it becomes invisible to the eyes of predators. The hindwings of moths normally have an elongated shape and real hooks keep them tightly strapped to the forewings: when the moth is at rest they normally fold like a roof over the body.

butterfly   moth

BELIEFS

While fairies are often pictured as delicate butterflies, in ancient cultures moths symbolize witches, as is often the case with nocturnal animals.

HABITS

Butterflies are typically diurnal, so we see them fly in the warmer hours of the day. Moths, despite having some very colorful diurnal representatives, usually have nocturnal habits and a duller coloration that allows them to blend into the surroundings during the day.

Moths normally have nocturnal habits.

3. BIG OR SMALL

Among both butterflies and moths we find some real giants.

QUEEN ALEXANDRA'S BIRDWING

The female of the Queen Alexandra's birdwing (*Ornithoptera alexandrae*) can reach the length of 3 in (8 cm) and a wingspan of 11 in (28 cm), compared to the male's maximum wingspan of 7.8 in (20 cm) and wing height of 7 in (18 cm).

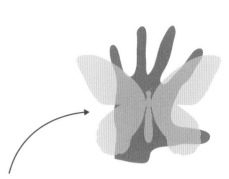

The Queen Alexandra's birdwing is larger than the palm of an adult man's hand.

♀

Female

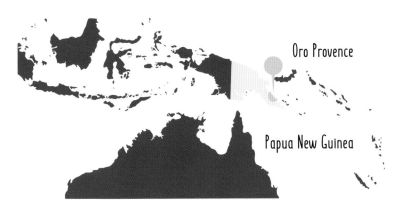

Oro Provence

Papua New Guinea

Australia

The Queen Alexandra's birdwing lives only in the forest of Oro Province, in Papua New Guinea.

It was given its name in 1907 by the naturalist who discovered it, in honor of Queen Alexandra of Denmark.

♂

Male

ATLAS MOTH

With a body that can reach 2.3 in (6 cm) in length, a wingspan of almost 11.8 in (30 cm) and a height of 8.2 in (21 cm), the female of the Atlas Moth or Cobra Butterfly (*Attacus atlas*), which is actually a moth, is generally considered the largest lepidopteran.

Size compared to the hand of an adult man.

WHITE WITCH

The White Witch (*Thysania agrippina*) comes close to a 11.8 in (30 cm) wingspan and often surpasses the Atlas moth, but its wing height is "only" 6 in (15 cm).

HERCULES MOTH

The greatest wing surface belongs without doubt to the intensely elegant Hercules moth (*Coscinocera hercules*) that can reach a wingspan of almost 9.8 in (25 cm) and, thanks to the long tails on its hindwings, a good 10.2 in (26 cm) in height.

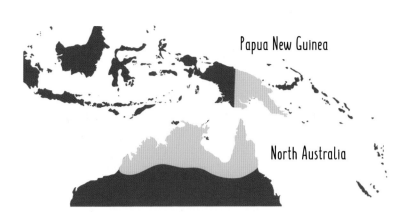

Papua New Guinea

North Australia

The huge Hercules moth lives in the warm climates of Northern Australia and Papua New Guinea.

GOLIATH BIRDWING

The second largest butterfly in the world is the Goliath birdwing *(Ornithoptera goliath)*, whose wingspan can reach 11 in (28 cm). It is native of New Guinea, where it is often raised for money: many foreign collectors in fact are willing to invest in this very colorful specimen.

The Goliath birdwing lives in Papua New Guinea.

Size compared to the hand of an adult man.

THE HEAVIEST BUTTERFLY

It's the Giant woodmoth *(Endoxyla cinerea)* that detains the title of heaviest lepidopteran, weighing a good 1 oz (30 grams)! Its gigantic caterpillar is a true nightmare for eucalyptus plants.

The Giant woodmoth is found in the territories of Eastern Australia and in New Zealand.

Australia

New Zealand

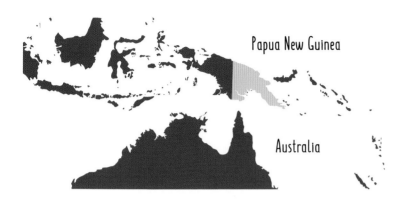

Papua New Guinea

Australia

THE SMALLEST BUTTERFLIES

The smallest butterflies belong to the Lycaenidae family, in particular the tiny Western pygmy blue *(Brephidium exilis)*, with a wingspan that barely exceeds 0.3 in (1 cm), is considered the smallest known butterfly.

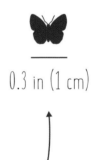

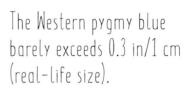

0.3 in (1 cm)

The Giant woodmoth's larvae dig holes in the wood of trees, where they build their nests until they emerge.

The Western pygmy blue barely exceeds 0.3 in/1 cm (real-life size).

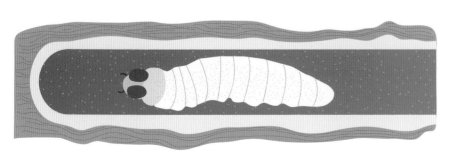

4. LEPIDOPTERANS IN THE WORLD

Researchers suppose that in little-explored regions there are still thousands of unknown lepidopterans, maybe as many as the 200,000 existing species, scattered on all the continents except Antarctica. Their geographical distribution is actually closely related to the vegetation on which they feed.

COSMOPOLITAN BUTTERFLIES

Some species are cosmopolitan, that is, they are found almost everywhere in the world, such as the European corn borer moth (*Ostrinianubilaslis*); others are endemic, that is, they live only on a particular island or mountain, such as the Eastern Orange Tip (*Anthocharis damone*). There are butterflies that can adapt to extreme environments, for example to 20,000 ft (6,000 m) of elevation on the Tibet mountains.

The Eastern Orange Tip is found only in the area of Mount Etna, in Sicily.

Butterflies are found all over the world, except in ice-cold Antarctica.

BIZARRE HABITATS

The Sloth moth (*Bradypodicola hahneli*) lives in a quite curious habitat: it spends its entire life among the hairs of sloths, feeding on the algae that develop in the fur of these South American animals.

5. ANATOMY OF A BUTTERFLY

Most butterflies feed on the nectar of flowers, an extremely sweet and highly energizing fluid. Plants are willing to produce and give up their nectar to insects in order to be pollinated and this is why they keep the precious nutrient safe in the deep regions at the base of their petals, so that the insects must "soil" themselves with pollen in order to reach it.

THE PROBOSCIS

Lepidopterans, just like great aristocrats, in order to reach the base of the corolla without getting too dirty have developed what is actually a straw: the mandibles have joined together and become longer to form a proboscis that coils under the head.

The Comet orchid

The proboscis is lacking in rare cases in which the adult lives so brief a life to not have the need to take in food, or in the case of certain moths whose proboscis is very short and therefore always kept uncoiled.

The length of the proboscis varies: it generally matches the length of the insect's body, but there are examples of it being three times as long! Such is the case of the little Hummingbird hawk-moth that can fly from one flower to the next with exceptionally fast wing beats, taking off in the air like a hummingbird.

THE GREATER DEATH'S HEAD HAWKMOTH

An opposite strategy is the one developed by the Greater death's head hawkmoth (*Acherontia atropos*), easy to recognize because of the skull-like pattern on its thorax: it has developed a somewhat short but very robust proboscis with which, during nocturnal hours, it can pierce the cells of beehives to reach the honey. It is so greedy for it that it will risk getting indigestion and, unable to move at that point, being killed by the bees despite the yellow and black coloration that makes it almost invisible inside the hive.

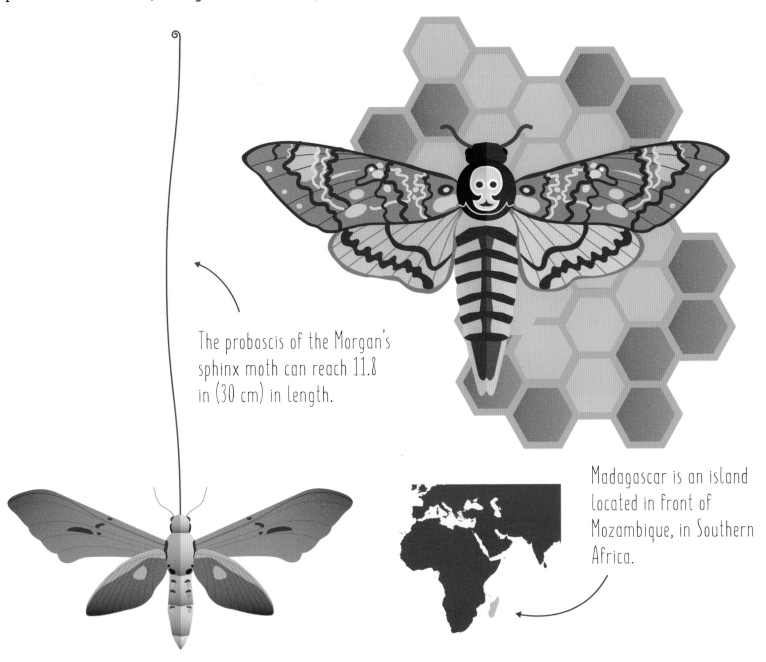

The proboscis of the Morgan's sphinx moth can reach 11.8 in (30 cm) in length.

Madagascar is an island located in front of Mozambique, in Southern Africa.

DARWIN AND THE MORGAN'S SPHINX MOTH

Who could be the pollinator of Madagascar's Comet orchid? This is the question posed by Darwin, the father of the evolution theory, when he saw this unique flower, in which the nectar was stored in the deepest region of the extremely long, typically modified petal that orchids have. It was only after more than 40 years that some researchers observed in Madagascar an African subspecies of the Morgan's sphinx moth (*Xanthopan morganii praedicta*), with a wingspan of 6 in (15 cm) and a proboscis that is nearly 11.8 in (30 cm) long!

In time, a co-evolution took place that has made the Morgan's sphinx moth the exclusive pollinator of the Comet orchid.

6. WINGS AND FLIGHT

In remote times, certain outgrowths of the thorax gave way to the first rudimentary insect wings. It is possible that they were useful to increase body surface and perhaps for thermoregulation, but they later became essential to colonize new territories, find rich food sources, locate a partner, and communicate.

WING MOVEMENT

Butterfly wings are not endowed with movement of their own: the wing beat is determined by the thorax that lowers and rises thanks to the inner muscle fasciae. At the base of the wings, though, there are muscles that allow a twisting motion: researchers have observed that butterflies during flight trace a complex eight-shaped pattern. A study on the *Vanessa atalanta* has shown the butterfly's ability to move its wings in at least six different ways.

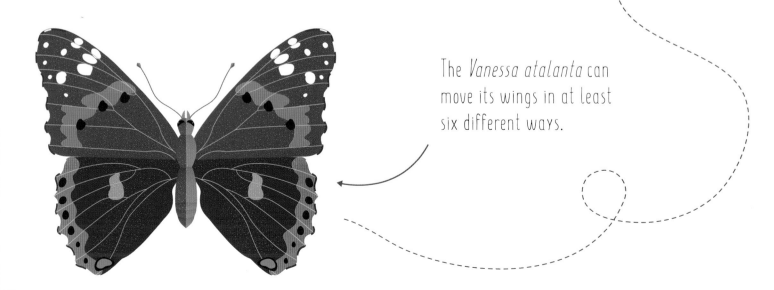

The *Vanessa atalanta* can move its wings in at least six different ways.

PIGMENTS AND LIGHT

The countless tiny scales that cover the wings of lepidopterans are in turn covered by even tinier structures capable of interacting with sunlight and giving unique iridescent colorations, resulting in a brilliant metallic effect. The colors of butterflies are in fact of two natures: they can be chemical if they are due to the presence of colored substances called pigments, or physical if they are the result of sunlight refraction. For example, the Blue morpho has just one pigment, black, but the structure of its wings makes it one of the most iridescent animals in nature.

The Blue morpho appears shimmering blue in the sunlight.

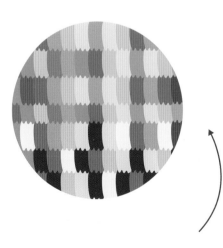

Butterfly wings are made up of tiny scales that are visible through a microscope.

7. SENSE ORGANS

Sight and smell are the senses most used by lepidopterans, for finding both food and a partner, so eyes and antennae are absolutely vital for their survival.

SIGHT

The simple eyes of caterpillars during metamorphosis are replaced by large compound eyes. Yes, because the eyes of butterflies, as those of insects in general, are made up of hundreds or even thousands of tiny eyes, called ommatidia, each of which captures a partial image of the surrounding environment. Despite having weaker eyesight than ours, the compound eye turns out to be an excellent instrument for expanding the visual field and locating a moving object with extreme precision.

In moths, the ommatidia are less distanced from each other than those of diurnal butterflies: thus they can have a brighter image in nocturnal hours and sometimes even see colors. Often on the head there are also two simple eyes, called ocelli, that are not capable of seeing shapes and colors but can perceive light intensity.

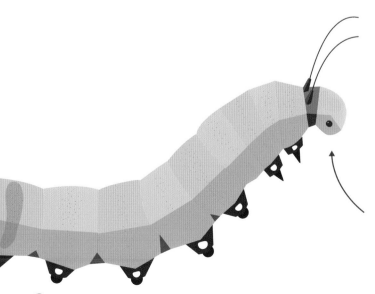

Simple eyes in caterpillars become compound eyes in butterflies.

Olfactory and touch
receptors

Compound eye

Touch and taste
receptors

Auditory receptors

HEARING

They don't have ears, they don't make sounds, except in extremely rare cases, so butterflies can't hear. Wrong! Compared to us, they tend to hear lower pitched sounds and to perceive ultrasounds, which we are not capable of hearing.

The vibrations that propagate through the air are detected by very sensitive hairs scattered all over their body. Some moths also possess eardrums made of a thin membrane stretched over an air-filled cavity, that is thus capable of vibrating. The position of these eardrums can vary a lot within the different families: at the base of the proboscis, near the joints of wings or legs, or on the first segments of the abdomen.

What a white
flower looks like
to man.

What the same
flower looks like
to a butterfly.

HOW DO BUTTERFLIES SEE?

Moreover, insects see colors differently from us: for example, many wild flowers that appear white are actually striped with a more or less intense pink to the eyes of bees and butterflies, which are capable of perceiving even ultraviolet light, invisible to human eye. We can distinguish a great number of color tones despite having 3 receptor classes, but a butterfly that lives in Australia and in South East Asia, the *Graphium sarpedon*, possesses 15 of them! It can therefore locate with precision the presence of tiny colored objects scattered among the leaves.

TASTE

As strange as it may seem, researchers have found that butterflies have their taste receptors on their feet! These sensors are of vital importance for the females who have to find the most suitable plants on which to lay their eggs.

TOUCH

Touch receptors are located on the antennae and on the legs. There are three types of receptors that add up the perception of pressure, sound, humidity, and temperature in the air. Particularly at the base of the antennae there is a specialized organ (Johnston's organ) that enables orientation during flight depending on this information.

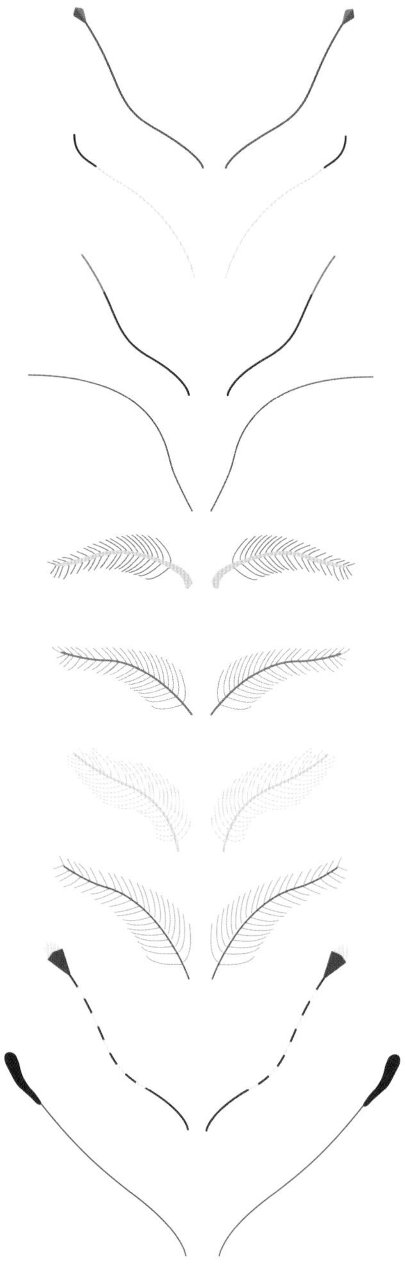

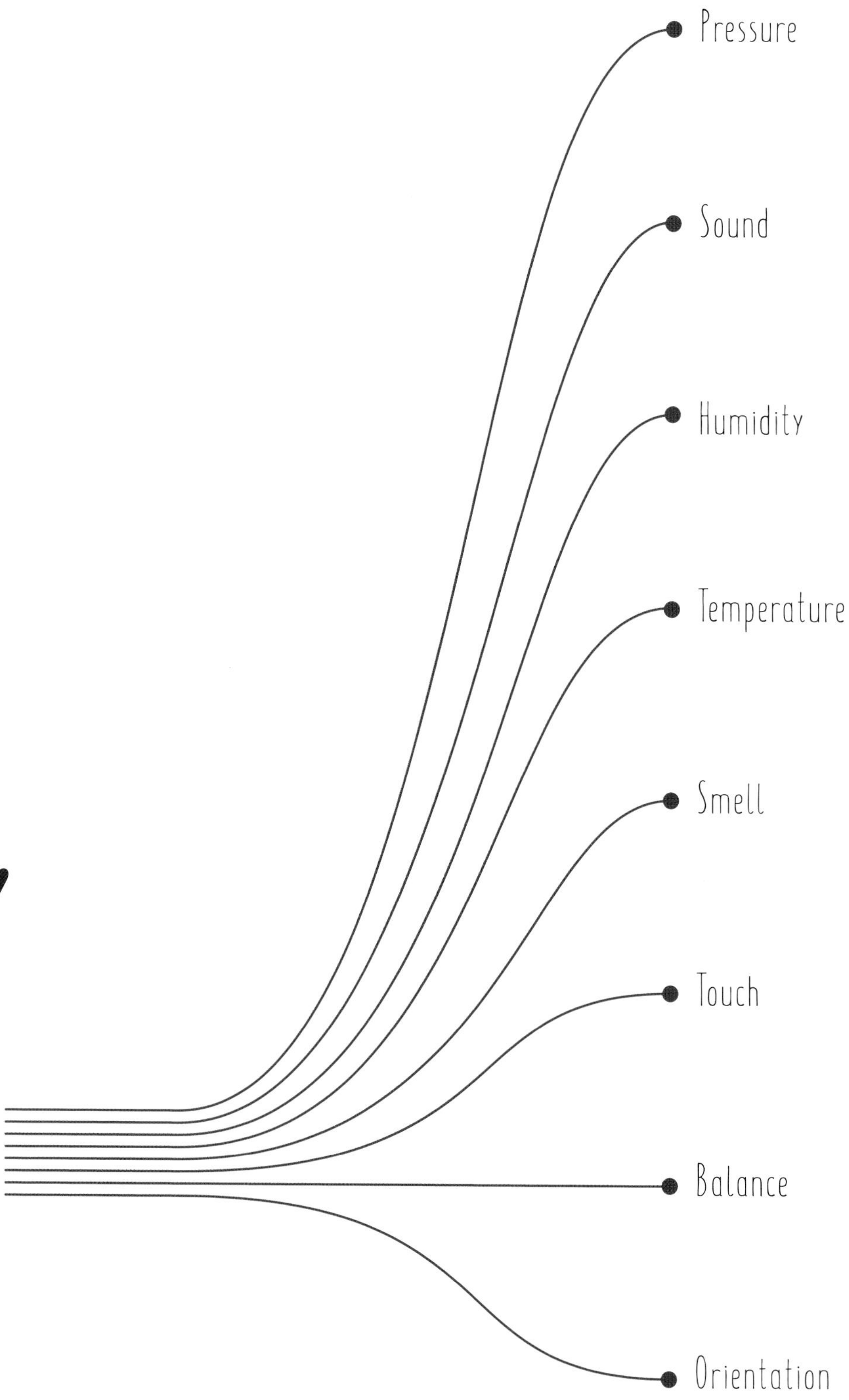

BUTTERFLY ANTENNAE
ARE USED TO DETERMINE

Pressure

Sound

Humidity

Temperature

Smell

Touch

Balance

Orientation

SMELL

To attract pollinators, plants have developed flowers equipped with enticing perfumes that can be perceived over considerable distances and even before coming into view.

But how can butterflies sense odor molecules if they don't have a nose? With their invaluable antennae, their sense organs for touch, balance and smell!

It is again the antennae that pick up the pheromones, particular chemical substances released by females to attract males even miles away. This is why males are equipped with even more complex and highly developed antennae.

8. HOW LONG DOES A BUTTERFLY LIVE?

Before turning into beautiful butterflies, lepidopterans must go through a complete metamorphosis that, starting from the egg and going through the caterpillar and chrysalis stages, will allow them to transform into adults capable of flight.

① Egg

Caterpillar

Pupa or chrysalis

Butterfly

① THE EGG

Once located a host or nurturer plant, the perfect food supply for her caterpillars, the female lays numerous eggs that are approximately 0.07-0.15 in (2-4 mm) in diameter. The eggs may be released singularly (Brown hairstreak) or in groups (Black-veined white) and secured to the leaves or stems with a glue-like substance.

Some have a very short adult life and may not be able to find a specific plant for their brood: this is the case of the Marbled white that lets its eggs fall in the fields as it flies so that they land on the ground.

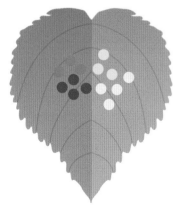

Butterfly eggs are very small and come in various colors depending on the species that lays them.

Depending on the species, it can take a few days, weeks, or even months for the egg to gradually darken and, in the end, a small larva hatches.

② THE CATERPILLAR

Its head is always highly developed and equipped with powerful jaws: it has an outstanding appetite! The caterpillar's task is to grow strong and stock up on substances that will be useful once it will have become a butterfly.

There are also caterpillars that feed on wood and dig tunnels in logs and branches. A peculiar case is that of predator caterpillars (*Lycaenididae*) that live in anthills catching the aphids that can be found there, as well as ants at the larval stage.

The outer "skin" of caterpillars, called cuticle, lacks elasticity and so as the insect grows it needs to molt it several times, just as if it were switching to a dress of a larger size. Molting takes place from two to maximum ten times. Near the mouth every caterpillar has tiny tube-like structures, called spinnerettes, from which silk is drawn.

During the molting period, the caterpillar attaches itself to a plant using a silk thread and swallows a great amount of air to inflate itself and break the cuticle, writhing itself out of it. In the meantime a new "skin" will have formed.

The caterpillar of the Arctic woolly bear moth lives in Greenland and is the most long-lived lepidopteran.

The legs, short and hooked at the extremity, are six, but on the abdomen there are also some "fake" legs that help the insect move by acting as suction cups.

"SPECIAL" CATERPILLARS

The life of a caterpillar can last from just over a week to up to several years. We can call "frozen caterpillar" the furry one belonging to the Arctic woolly bear moth (*Gynaephora groenlandica*): this larva, in fact, has merely the span of the Arctic tundra's short summer to grow, then it hibernates in a silk cocoon, surviving temperatures as low as -76°F (-60°C)!

When summer returns, it "thaws", resumes eating and so on for various years, living 95% of its life in hibernation.

③ THE PUPA

After having grown as much as possible, the caterpillar prepares to transform into a pupa or chrysalis. It stops eating and looks for a sheltered place, hanging from a branch or even underground, as is the case with the *Sphingidae*. To insulate itself from the outside environment, it produces a rubbery substance which, as it dries, forms a casing whose shape and color differs among the various families.

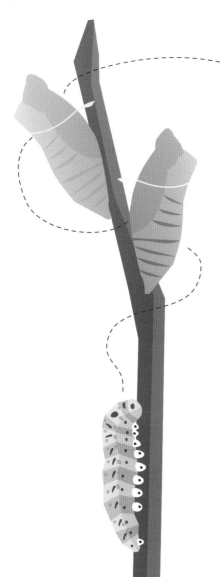

The Machaon has a summer chrysalis, green in color, and a winter one that is beige.

A butterfly can take from a few minutes to an hour to spread its wings.

Moths, in particular, can further protect the chrysalis by means of a cocoon made with a thread of silk, sometimes wrapped in a leaf or covered with plant matter. Protected by the casing, the caterpillar will slowly transform into a beautiful butterfly.

This phase can last from a little less than two weeks to various months, if it has to spend the winter months in this state. In some species, such as the *Papilio machaon*, there are two types of chrysalis, a summer one, which is green in color, that emerges after about fifteen days, and a beige one that winters and transforms into a butterfly the following spring.

④ THE ADULT, THE BUTTERFLY

When the pupa darkens and it is possible to get a glimpse of the butterfly's definite structure within, the "emerging" from the cocoon is about to take place: the membrane is torn and the butterfly starts to come out.

Once free, tired and still wet, it breathes in a great amount of air to extend the wings before they harden, otherwise they would remain deformed. In a period of time that ranges from just a few minutes to one hour it is ready to take off: its metamorphosis is complete!

The duty of the adult is to have offspring: it must find a partner, mate, find a place to lay the eggs and... begin again an entire new life cycle!

In some species all this has to be done in very little time: from two days to a week.

To speed up the reproductive phase, females are born bearing eggs that are already mature; their pheromones can be picked up from miles away and the eggs can be left on numerous plants or even to fall on the ground.

The Blue morpho's realtively long life depends on its fruit-based diet.

The European peacock butterfly can live up to eight months.

HOW LONG DOES A BUTTERFLY LIVE?

The species equipped with proboscis can normally live a couple of weeks or a few months: among the most long-lived, Caligo and Morpho, that adore very ripe fruit, or the Heliconius butterflies, that feed also on pollen. By adding to their diet highly nutritious foods, they can live over 6 months. Then there are species that spend the winter as adults in sheltered places, including houses, without eating, in a sort of lethargy, and that therefore live many months, such as the European peacock butterfly or the Hummingbird hawk-moth. An exceptional case is that of the Monarch butterfly that can reach 9 months of life and accomplish long migrations.

9. MATING AND REPRODUCTION

The breeding season of lepidopterans corresponds to their entire adult life. Male butterflies spend most of the day seeking for a mate: the visual approach is key, while olfactory stimuli are used later on. In some species, males follow precise colors, while in others they recognize flight techniques.

COURTSHIP

Therefore, it is often possible to witness spectacular dances on behalf of the males or of both partners, during which certain pheromones are released. Males may follow directly the chosen female or wait for her in areas particularly sheltered from predators: in both cases they will eventually have to fight off rivals.

HOW MOTHS BREED

Instead, in the case of moths, the 'sweethearts' meet thanks to pheromones released by the females and perceived by the sensors located on the antennae of males. These chemical substances, detectable miles away, are specific to each species.

In some species, the females, with an extremely short adult life, start to produce chemical substances to attract males when they are still in the chrysalis stage, so as to be able to choose a male as soon as they start to emerge.

The *Astraptes fulgerator* reproduces without the need of a partner.

GYNANDROMORPHISM

As in the case of other insects, there are butterflies capable of reproduction without the presence of a male, that is, by parthenogenesis. In this case, from unfecundated eggs only females practically identical to their mother will be born (for example, *Astraptes fulgerator*).

10. SOCIAL BEHAVIOR

They weigh a few onces, yet they can fly for more than 4,300 mi (7,000 km) going from the Great Lakes, on the border between Canada and USA, to the valleys of Mexico: these are the Monarch butterflies.

MIGRATIONS

Orange with black and white decorations, they gather in Fall in huge storms, ready to migrate to places where the winter is milder and remain there in a state of semi-hibernation.

During migration, Monarch butterflies can be admired hanging from tree trunks in clusters.

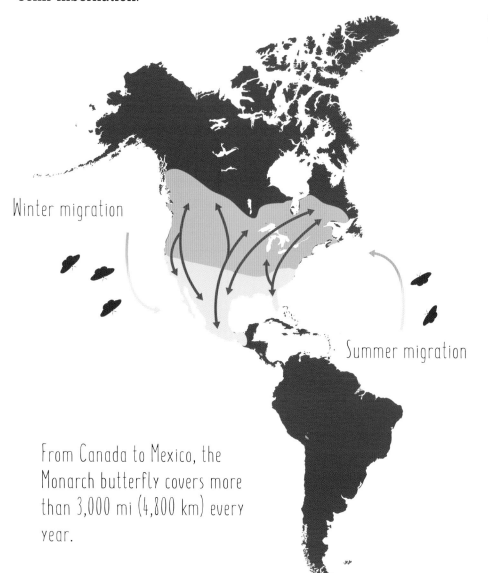

Winter migration

Summer migration

From Canada to Mexico, the Monarch butterfly covers more than 3,000 mi (4,800 km) every year.

Once the temperature starts to rise, they are capable of returning whence they came and start to reproduce. During the summer, three generations of butterflies succeed one another until the great-nieces and nephews of the butterflies that migrated previously are ready to leave again.

This new generation is capable of following the same routes of their ancestors, sometimes reaching the very same tree of their predecessors.

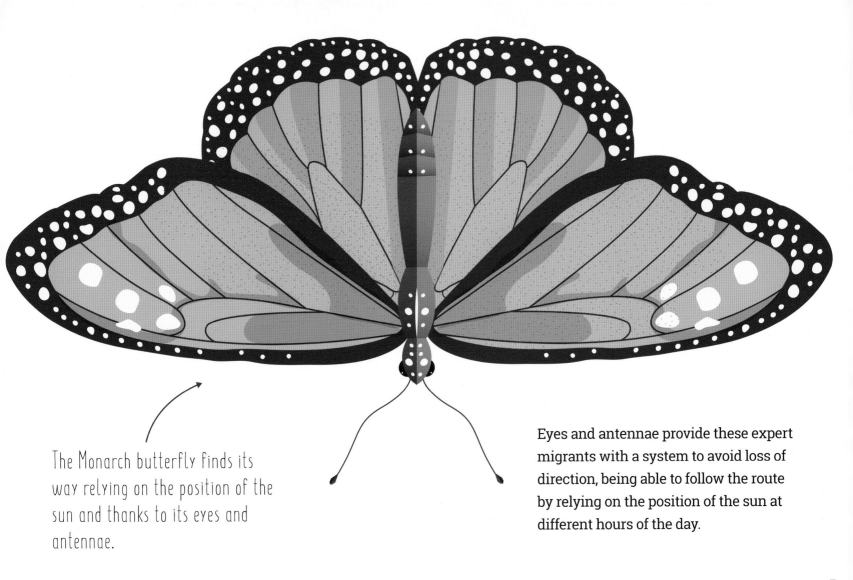

The Monarch butterfly finds its way relying on the position of the sun and thanks to its eyes and antennae.

Eyes and antennae provide these expert migrants with a system to avoid loss of direction, being able to follow the route by relying on the position of the sun at different hours of the day.

OTHER MIGRANTS, THE PAINTED LADY

In Europe, the Painted Lady *(Vanessa cardui* or *Cinthia cardui)* weighs a little more than 0.03 oz (1 gram), has a brain as big as a pinhead, but is capable of flying a distance of 9,300 mi/15,000 km (twice that of the Monarch butterfly) at a speed of 28 mph (45 km/h), making the most of the winds and crossing the Mediterranean Sea.

Fall migration

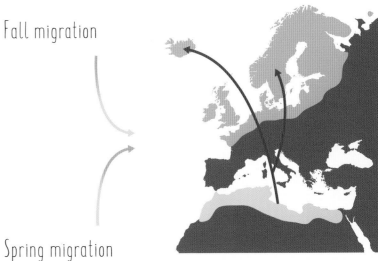

Spring migration

In Fall it reaches North Africa, where it reproduces and winters in the form of chrysalis; in spring, the newly emerged adults take off for Northern Europe, including Iceland, where several generations succeed them.

Despite having different patterns, they share the same colors of Monarch butterflies, but during their migrations they fly at about 1,600 ft (500 m) in the air and so we are unable to spot them.

THE BUTTERFLY VALLEY

In the Petaloudes Valley or Butterfly Valley on the island of Rhodes, Greece, thousands of butterflies gather during the summer months.

It's a very narrow valley, delimited by steep mountain sides, rich in water and with a thick evergreen vegetation that keeps the sunlight from penetrating the undergrowth: the result is a temperature considerably lower than that of the surrounding area.

Here thousands of Jersey Tiger moths (*Euplagia* o *Panaxia quadripunctaria*) come to spend the sweltering summer months without eating and, instead, using the supplies gathered when they were caterpillars as they wait for cooler temperatures to arrive so that they can reproduce.

This moth's black and white forewings, when at rest, cover the red-orange hindwings: this is why it's spectacular to see them fly, but the whistling or hand-clapping of the tourists are received as a serious threat and the shock causes the death or the lack of reproduction of many of them.

MOTHS AND LIGHT

During summer evenings we often see moths twirling around street lamps or light bulbs, sometimes flying into the source of light and burning themselves.

This happens because artificial light makes their sense of direction go haywire. They have always stayed on course using the moon and the stars, but a lamp is extremely near; light is radiated in all directions and for the poor moths this means serious trouble!

11. CAMOUFLAGE AND DEFENSE STRATEGIES

To us giants, butterflies seem fragile and vulnerable: but actually, to outdo their predators, they have developed many strategies to use during the various stages of their development.

Camouflage is the phenomenon by which animals can "hide" by imitating the colors and shapes of their surroundings or other similar animals. Different tactics are available, though, depending on the species.

The caterpillar of *Ascotis selenaria* looks like the green twigs of plants.

CRYPSIS

This is the most common case, when butterlies tend to blend in, or make themselves cryptic, with the surface on which they land; an example of this are the moths that "disappear" when they rest on tree bark or green caterpillars among blades of grass.

A special case is that of the superb Glass-winged butterfly of South America, that possesses transparent wings with dark veins. Predator birds see leaves and flowers as if through a glass and cannot focus on the possible prey.

BUTTERFLIES OR LEAVES?

Some species can trick predators by taking on the perfect likeness of leaves, twigs, or other natural elements. Examples of this are caterpillars of *Lycia hirtaria* or of *Ascotis selenaria* that look like real plant twigs.

The wings of the Glass-winged butterfly make it invisible to predators.

WARNING COLORS

Other species opt for bright and lively colors: these are toxic or "undesirable" animals that are warning their potential predators. This coloration, known as aposematic, can be paired with repellent odors, as in the case of the Machaon, or terror-instilling behavior, using eye-like markings as well.

The Kallima or Indian Oakleaf (or Dead leaf butterfly) has wings that in flight appear brightly colored and present an original shape. When it lands and its wings close on its back we can see that not only the color, but also its whole shape imitates a dead leaf complete with stalk.

The lappet is a moth that, as its Latin name *quercifolia* suggests, feeds mainly on oaks and imitates to perfection the dead leaves of these plants.

The "Harpy" caterpillar scares its predators with its menacing appearance.

Some butterflies imitate perfectly the tree leaves on which they rest.

For example, the green and black "Harpy" caterpillar of the Puss moth, if disturbed, raises its head showing red markings, just as the two filaments it has attached behind; if its threat goes unheeded, it is forced to spray formic acid.

The adult Polyxena butterfly (*Zerinthia polixena*) presents warning colors because it is not edible to birds: it's their larvae that accumulate toxic substances by feeding on poisonous plants.

41

THE OWL BUTTERFLY

The Owl butterfly (*Caligo*) has eye-like markings on the lower region of its hindwings: when resting, it looks as if each eye, one per side, is staring out at nobody in particular, but as soon as the butterfly thinks a threat is at hand, it positions itself upside down and opens its wings, transforming itself into the head of a fearsome owl and frightening away lizards and small birds.

IMITATION AND MIMICRY

Some butterflies that are attractive to predators imitate a model, that is, a different species equipped with chemical defenses. This is the case of the Monarch butterfly that, being toxic, is imitated in shape and color by the Viceroy butterfly (Batesian mimicry). In order for the trick to work, it is important that the number of Viceroy butterflies be considerably less than the Monarch butterflies: once a little bird tastes a Monarch, it will never again capture one nor any other that resembles it!

Viceroy butterfly

Monarch butterfly

The Postman butterfly and the Heliconius are both poisonous

Instead, between the Postman butterflies and Heliconius there is a different relationship because the two species imitate each other, despite their being both poisonous: therefore they boost their defense system (Müllerian mimicry).

THE PEPPERED MOTH

A special case is that of the not very eye-catching Peppered moth that has become very famous, to the point of being mentioned in all science books in school as an example of evolution brought about by natural selection. Biston betularia – this is its scientific name – is whitish and blends in well with the light color of birch trunks which are partly covered by lichens.

At the beginning of the 19th century, a mutation caused the appearance of darker colored moths as well, which survived in small numbers because predatory birds could easily spot them.

Things changed in the vicinity of large cities in the wake of the Industrial Revolution because, due to the smog derived from coal, the lichens died and the barks of tree blackened: very soon the numbers of the two types of Biston changed and the darker moths increased considerably to the detriment of the lighter ones. The use of "clean" forms of energy is bringing things back to the original situation.

OTHER WEAPONS OF DEFENSE

There are those who are capable of disguising themselves, instilling fright and storing toxic substances, but there are a few who have been able to develop highly ingenious systems of defense. Bats are among the nocturnal moths' most feared predators: they can move and get the necessary information concerning obstacles and prey thanks to the echo of the ultrasounds they emit.

The Tiger moth emits ultrasounds to defend itself from predators.

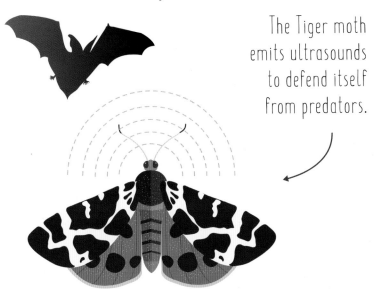

The Tiger moth (Arctia caja), a lepidopteran of the Arizona desert has learned how to use the same weapon by emitting up to 4500 ultrasonic clicks per second and creating around itself a sound barrier.

12. BUTTERFLIES AND MAN

Beautiful and graceful, butterflies are essential to the pollination of countless botanical species and constitute one of the fulcrums of the food system. Some lepidopterans, like the Spurge hawk-moth, are used by man in his attempt through biological methods to keep under control invasive weeds. Many species are an important part of traditional cuisine in some countries and the silkworm represents a remarkable economic resource.

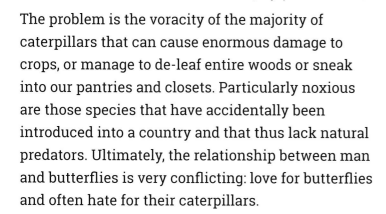

VORACIOUS CATERPILLARS

The problem is the voracity of the majority of caterpillars that can cause enormous damage to crops, or manage to de-leaf entire woods or sneak into our pantries and closets. Particularly noxious are those species that have accidentally been introduced into a country and that thus lack natural predators. Ultimately, the relationship between man and butterflies is very conflicting: love for butterflies and often hate for their caterpillars.

UNDESIRED GUESTS

The Codling moth (*Cydia pomonella*) represents one of the most damaging to apple farming, but also to pear and walnut cultivations as well. The larva feeds on the fruit, digging tunnels inside it and causing huge crop loss.

The larva of the Codling moth is an insatiable caterpillar that feeds on fruit.

HUMAN DEFENSES AGAINST PARASITES

Man has implemented many techniques to fight parasitic larvae: the ever more powerful poisonous substances scattered in the environment are dangerous and are little by little being surpassed by more advanced techniques.

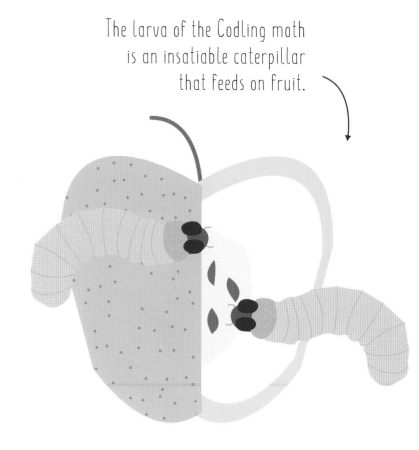

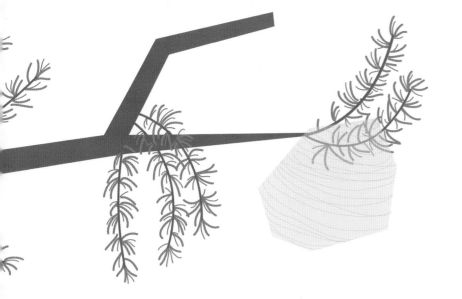

The Pine processionary builds a large nest on the branches of pine trees.

THE PINE PROCESSIONARY

The name of the Pine processionary (*Thaumetopoea pityocampa*) derives from the caterpillars' act of proceeding in a single file, as in a procession, when moving from one branch to the next, leaving it bare, or on the ground when they bury themselves to change into chrysalides.

Their jaws are exceptionally strong, capable of chewing pine needles from the day they are born. We can easily observe their silk nests in which they spend the winter too.

The adults are moths lacking mouthparts that live maximum two days: the females immediately look for the branch on which to lay a mass of approximately 300 eggs.

The caterpillars of the Pine processionary moth possess hairs that are extremely irritating to man and domestic animals.

THE COMMON CLOTHES MOTH

Among the various species of Tineola that love to use our kitchens to find warmth and plenty of food, there are those that prefer to feed on our clothes, either of wool or leather, leaving them with holes!

To get rid of these little moths, we can wash our clothes at a temperature over 104°F (40°C), or leave them in the freezer for a month, or expose them to sunlight or, in any case, airing out our closets and placing lavender or cedar-scented bags inside them.

BUTTERFLIES FOR LUNCH!

Among lepidopterans, silkworms are considered a traditional "street food" in China, while in Thailand, Cambodia and Oceania many other species are added to dishes for their high protein content.

13. CONSERVATION

Researchers have realized that over the past years the number of butterflies has been steadily decreasing, causing a loss of scarcely pollinated plant species and a consistent loss of biodiversity. A more in-depth study of their biology and behavior can aid in the development of plans for their protection.

PESTICIDES AND NATURAL REMEDIES

Extensive farming has determined a greater use of pesticides, which kill both the species considered noxious as well as the others. Agronomists are therefore looking for less invasive and more focused methods, while legislators are banning the use of particularly toxic substances and are allowing the creation of protected areas of particular interest.

THE LOSS OF BUTTERLIES

As for all animals, one of the first causes is due to environmental changes that determine a reduction of suitable areas for reproduction, feeding and finding shelter throughout the different stages of their metamorphosis. For this reason, for years now biologists have been successfully working on the creation of "ecological passageways" made with wild plants and shrubs, which are used as partitions between cultivated fields.

THE APOLLO BUTTERFLY

The protection of the mountain environment has its symbol in the Apollo butterfly, the first invertebrate in Europe to be included in the Red List of endangered animals.
In fact it needs mountain slopes with plenty of sunlight and flowers even at over 5,500 ft (1,700 m) of elevation.

Some particularly endangered species, especially those living in restricted areas, are being raised in protected areas in order to release adults capable of breeding in the wild.

The Apollo butterfly, which risks extinction, is the symbol of the protection of mountain environments.

Many particularly colorful tropical species are contributing to the sustainable development in certain countries, where they are raised and sent as chrysalides to greenhouses or butterfly houses scattered all over the world. This promotes learning and involvement on behalf of visitors, besides increasing the number of butterflies that, in part, are released in their distribution area.

14. THE SILKWORM

The Silkmoth (*Bombyx mori*) is a moth originally from Central East Asia whose caterpillar devours mulberry leaves incessantly, day and night. The 4 consecutive molts that it undergoes spell out its life, dividing it in five periods called "instars". It is only when it molts that it stops eating.

The silk thread of the silkworm is used as protection during its trasformation from chrysalis to butterfly.

Once growth is completed, the larva climbs on a twig and, using glands located at the sides of its mouth, it starts to draw a thread of silk. After 3 or 4 days the cocoon is finally finished: 20 or 30 concentric layers of protein substances have been built with a single extremely long and continuous thread.

There are many different breeds of this species, which, having been raised by man for thousands of years, are no longer capable of living in the wild.

THE HISTORY OF SILK

According to a legend, in 3000 B.C. Xi Ling Shih, wife of the emperor, noticed a caterpillar during one of her walks, petted it, and a thread of silk wrapped itself around her finger, forming a little cocoon. The empress decided to use that soft thread to make magnificent fabrics.

However, some archeological findings apparently date the beginning of silk cloth farming back 6000 years near the Blue River.

The silkworm takes 3 to 4 days to build its silk cocoon.

Thanks to merchants, the qualities of this cloth were soon appreciated by the ancient Egyptians and Romans, but the Chinese emperors managed to keep the knowledge of sericulture secret for a long time.

Reportedly, it was only in 550 A.D. that several monks succeeded in smuggling out some Bombyx eggs and, 500 years later, the know-how finally reached Italy, where silk manufacturing greatly developed.

SILKWORM FARMING

That is, raising silkworms; it begins between April and May, when mulberry leaves have fully developed. The small caterpillars are placed on frequently cleaned trellises and fed fresh mulberry leaves, given to them several times a day after the third molt.

The room that houses them must be adequately ventilated and the temperature must be kept as close as possible to 77°F (25°C).

If the metamorphosis should reach completion, the moth would pierce the cocoon, cutting the thread. This is the reason why silkworm farmers kill the chrysalides in purposely designed dryers and then immerge them in boiling water to unroll the silk thread. In China chrysalides are consumed as food.

15. RAISING BUTTERFLIES

We all can help butterflies return to considerable numbers and in this way protect the flora and the environment that surround us. Though a demanding task, raising butterflies is very rewarding.

KITS FOR RAISING BUTTERFLIES

There are learner kits available for beginners: inside there are a few eggs or caterpillars of a certain species, food or instructions on the plants they feed on, a plastic box in which to raise the larvae, and a structure made with mesh walls in which to allow the adults to free themselves of the cocoon and be released outside.

To create a real farm, the following is required: suitable containers, specific food, a thermostat, a humidifier and, finally, the eggs of the chosen lepidopteran.

DIFFERENT TYPES OF TERRARIUMS

They are needed depending on the different age and characteristics of the surroundings. The eggs must be placed in small plastic boxes so that they don't dry out. As for the other stages, it will be necessary to get a number of somewhat large terrariums, which should be easy to keep clean on the inside.

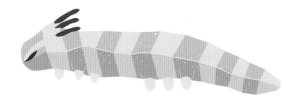

The options available are common fauna-boxes, sold in pet stores, that are better at maintaining humidity but provide little ventilation; or, using some wooden pieces and mesh, we can build by ourselves our caterpillars' home: in this case it would be wise to add a zipper to one of the walls to allow easy access and remember to mist some water frequently.

SETTING UP AND CARING FOR THE TERRARIUM

For caterpillars at their first stage of development, it is important to place some paper towel on the bottom and some shredded leaves of the host plant.

After the first molt, it would be better to enlarge the size of the terrarium and use whole twigs of plants that, once put in a container with water, securing the container's opening so as to keep the caterpillars from drowning, should reach the ground allowing the caterpillars to climb on them. Sometimes it is necessary to put the plants in a vase within the terrarium.

When moving or cleaning it, it is important to be careful not to touch the little caterpillars with your hands but only with a soft and fine brush!

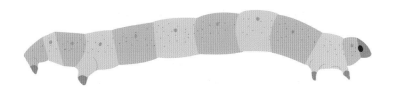

With pupas, some small branches on which to attach will suffice, but for many species the best thing to do is to place a thick layer of peat on the bottom. At this point, by keeping the small branches inside as supports and misting water to maintain the humidity, all that is left to do is wait for the adult butterflies to appear!

16. BUTTERFLY GARDENS

If you have a garden or a terrace, you can invite butterflies over to lunch, contributing to their safeguard and making these outdoor areas much more attractive.

It's easier to add plants with bright colors and with scents that attract adults, whereas it can be more difficult to satisfy the caterpillars. For this reason, if there is enough space, it would be good to destine at least a small part of it to the growth of wild flora. In any case, the first rule is to avoid as much as possible insecticides.

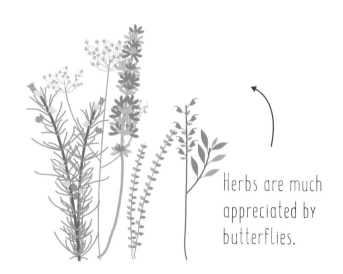

Herbs are much appreciated by butterflies.

HERBS

Plants that are useful in the kitchen and excellent for attracting butterflies are herbs, that is plants such as rosemary, sage, marjoram, verbena, lavender, or thyme.

Hummingbird hawk-moth

PLANTS THAT ATTRACT BUTTERFLIES

With their colors, but especially with the intense perfumes that they emanate and that can be perceived from far away, flowers of certain botanical varieties have an irresistible appeal to lepidopterans.

Some examples are the various species of Lantana, Lilac, Verbena, Sweet Alyssum, Valerian, Spirea, Pyracantha, Zinnia and Buddleia that, known as the "butterfly bush" is a must in our garden, despite it not being part of our flora.

HOST PLANTS

Some interactions are more specific, thus honeysuckle flowers attract the *Sphingidae*, which are equipped with a very long proboscis (hummingbird hawk-moth, *Macroglossa stellatarum*).

Butterflies and moths search for sources of food, but above all they look for host plants on which to lay their eggs, therefore in a small area we can help bring about the birth of new butterflies. Examples of synergy between plants and caterpillars are:

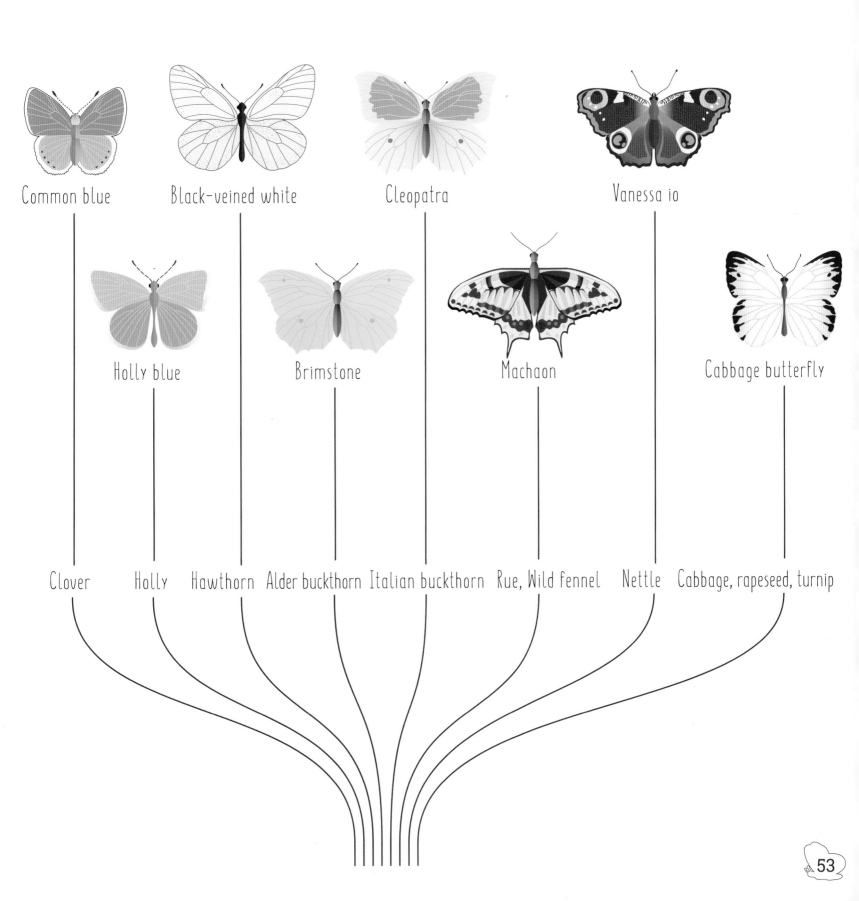

Common blue

Black-veined white

Cleopatra

Vanessa io

Holly blue

Brimstone

Machaon

Cabbage butterfly

Clover   Holly   Hawthorn   Alder buckthorn   Italian buckthorn   Rue, Wild fennel   Nettle   Cabbage, rapeseed, turnip

17. MYTHS AND LEGENDS

In the collective unconscious the butterfly has always been very fascinating: it flies showing colorful wings and, above all, it is capable of transforming itself by going through metamorphosis. For this reason, as far back as in ancient times, myths and legends concerned with the life cycle and beauty began to develop.

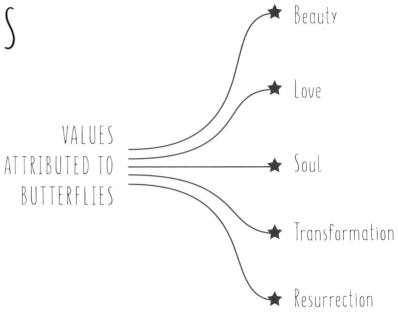

VALUES ATTRIBUTED TO BUTTERFLIES

★ Beauty
★ Love
★ Soul
★ Transformation
★ Resurrection

BUTTERFLIES IN ANCIENT GREECE

The myths of Psyche and Hypnos belong to ancient Greece. Psyche, which means both butterfly and "animating spirit" or soul, was the name of a beautiful princess who out of jealousy was persecuted by Aphrodite, goddess of beauty, but in the end manages to marry her son Eros, god of love.

The god of sleep Hypnos, pictured with butterfly wings on his head, also was in charge of transporting the dead into the afterworld together with his brother Thanatos, god of death.

The myth of Eros and Psyche is represented in the sculpture of artist Antonio Canova.

These myths were later picked up by different cultures, therefore both in ancient Egypt and in Celtic tradition or in Japanese symbolism the butterfly represents beauty, delicate love, but also the soul and transformation after death.

In Christian religion it is a symbol of resurrection, as it is also of love and, in the Middle Ages, angels were pictured as butterflies.

SUPERSTITION

In different countries the butterfly can represent a positive sign or a bad omen, even depending on the different colors. In China it brings joy, abundance and health.

In the Anglo-Saxon tradition the first butterfly seen in the morning announces good luck if it is white; it brings good luck throughout one's life if it is pink, and predicts disease if it is yellow.

If a white butterfly enters the house, the interpretations can vary quite a lot: it can bring death, good fortune, or simply heat!

In the Anglo-Saxon tradition, if the first butterfly seen in the morning is pink, it brings good luck for one's entire life.

THE LEGEND OF THE WHITE BUTTERFLY

The legend tells of an old Japanese man that no one ever saw in the company of a woman.

When he fell ill, his sister and his nephew came to take care of him. One day a white butterfly entered the house several times and would land on the old man's pillow and then fly away. The nephew tried to follow it and the butterfly rested on a tomb and then disappeared. On the tombstone he found the word Akiko.

The boy told his mother and she understood. Akiko had been the old man's fiancé many years before and had died a few days before their wedding. He had moved to live near her tomb in order to go visit her every day and the day he no longer was able to go, the soul of his beloved had gone to visit him at the moment of his death!

THE LEGEND OF THE BLUE BUTTERFLY

The legend of the blue butterfly tells of two very intelligent sisters that would always ask their widowed father questions that were too complicated.

So he decided to send them to a wise man to learn from him. Since the wise man always answered their questions, the sisters decided to trick him.

One of them captured a blue butterfly and planned to ask the wise man if the butterfly in her hand was alive or dead: if he were to say alive, she would crush it; if he were to say dead, she would free it, so the wise man would be wrong either way.

But his answer to her question was:

"It depends on you because it is in your hands."

The butterfly symbolizes our life whose present and future are in our hands.

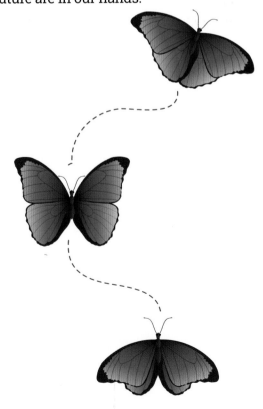

18. LIST OF BUTTERFLIES ENCOUNTERED IN THIS BOOK

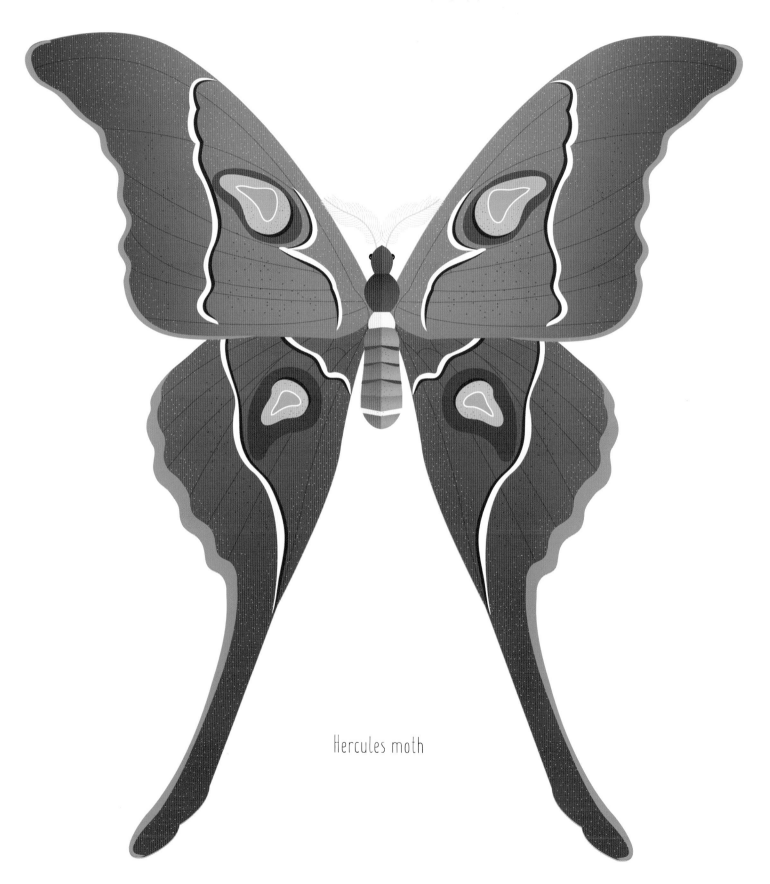

Hercules moth

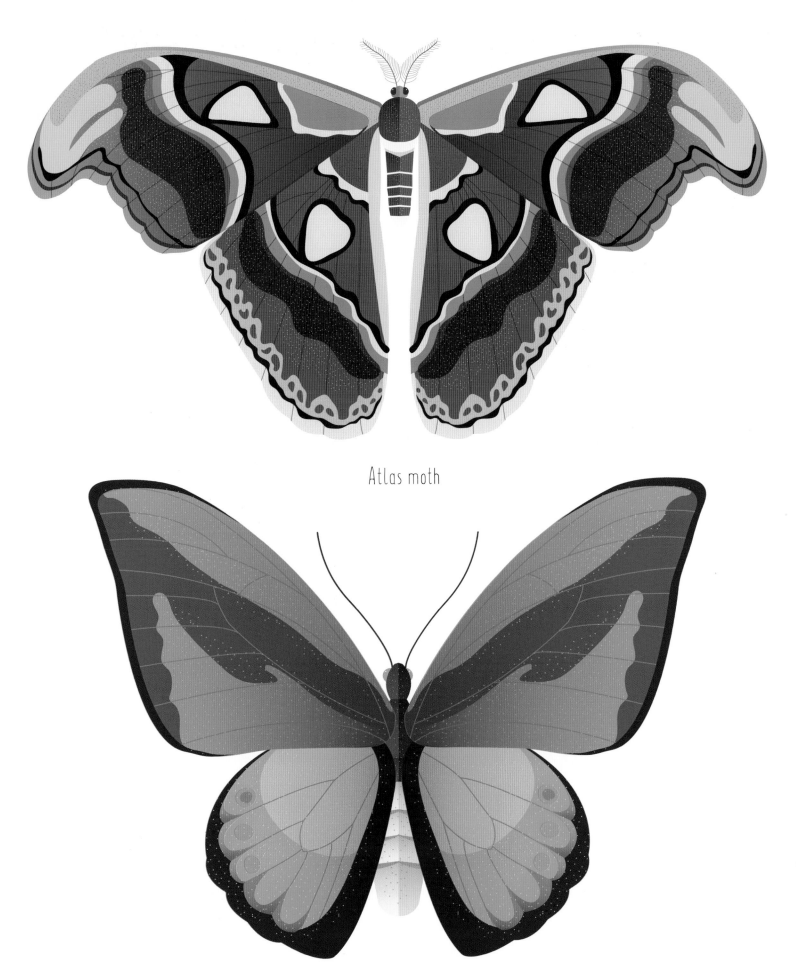

Atlas moth

Goliath birdwing

White witch

Western pygmy blue

Queen Alexandra's ♀
birdwing

Common blue

Queen Alexandra's ♂
birdwing

Holly blue

Owl butterfly

Morgan's sphynx moth

Greater death's head hawk moth

Monarch

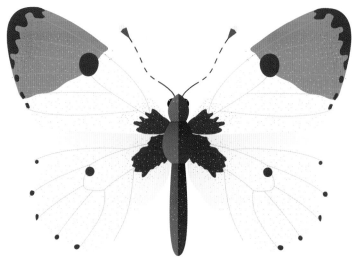

Eastern Orange Tip

Viceroy

Papilio phorcas

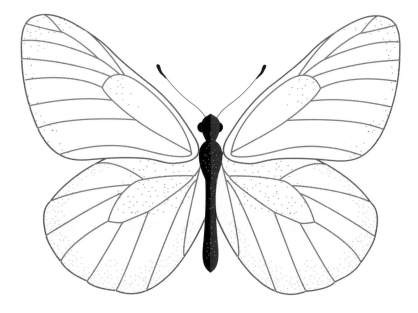

Black-veined white

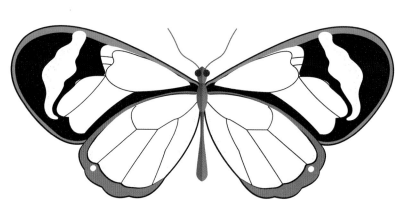

Glass-winged butterfly

Blue morpho

Brimstone

Astraptes fulgerator

Cleopatra

Cabbage butterfly

Machaon

Jersey tiger moth

Painted lady

Tiger moth

Vanessa atalanta

Apollo butterfly

European peacock

Heliconius butterfly

Peppered moth

Puss moth

Postman butterfly

Sloth moth

Marbled white

Giant wood moth

Rita Mabel Schiavo

After graduating in Biological Sciences specializing in Natural Sciences at the Università Statale di Milano, her studies have continued in the field of herpetology and eco-ethology.
She is one of the founding partners and administrators of ADM – Associazione Didattica Museale and of ADMaiora, which are involved in teaching in museums, natural parks, sanctuaries and exhibits.
In recent years she has written, several books for White Star Kids.

Giulia De Amicis

Born in Milan in 1986, after earning her Master's Degree in Design, she started to work as information designer and illustrator for small studios, newspapers and ENGOs. Over the years she has studied and lived in Italy, Spain, India and Greece. She currently works and lives in Brighton, England. In the past years she has realized several books for White Star Kids.

WSKids
WHITE STAR KIDS

White Star Kids® is a registered trademark property of White Star s.r.l.

© 2018 White Star s.r.l.
Piazzale Luigi Cadorna, 6 - 20123 Milan, Italy
www.whitestar.it

Translation: Ellisse s.a.s. di Sergio Abate & C.

ISBN 978-88-544-1275-0
  2 3 4 5 6   23 22 21 20 19

Printed in Italia by Rotolito S.p.A. - Seggiano di Pioltello (Milan)

Graphic Design
Valentina Figus